Whispers
Over a Brewing
Dawn

Poems by Marial Awendit

First published in Great Britain in 2022 by:

Carnelian Heart Publishing Ltd

Suite A

82 James Carter Road

Mildenhall

Suffolk

IP28 7DE

UK

www.carnelianheartpublishing.co.uk

©Marial Awendit 2022

Paperback ISBN 978-1-914287-21-3

Ebook ISBN 978-1-914287-22-0

All rights reserved. No part of this publication may be reproduced, stored in a retrieval system or transmitted in any form or by any means, electronic, mechanical, photocopying, recording or otherwise without prior written permission from the publisher.

Editors: Dzikamayi Chando & Samantha Rumbidzai Vazhure

Cover layout:

Daniel Mutendi

Book interior:

Typeset by Carnelian Heart Publishing Ltd

Layout and formatting by DanTs Media

Table of Contents

x	Prologue
1.	Glow
2.	How a Firefly Dies
3.	national misery
4.	Sacrifice
5.	Neck
6.	Hospital Lights
7.	Bites
8.	history
9.	Fractions
10.	tragedies
11.	boat
12.	love
13.	coil
14.	Yard
15.	Ode to Nothingness
17.	I Adore
18.	Somehow
19.	Cloths
20.	Kites
21.	Soul
22.	Ode to a Pull
23.	Pine Trees in the Rain
24.	At Mulago Cancer Ward
25.	Why Did You Let Them Tell You
26.	I sense Their Signals
27.	Nothing
28.	Ode to Nationalism
29.	Lenses

30.	Diary Scribbles
31.	Passions with a War Veteran
32.	Just Watch Me
33.	Moths
34.	Diabolism
35.	The Universe
36.	Audition
37.	Soothing
38.	Winged by Time
39.	Aroma
40.	Place
41.	Ode to the Maker of the Nile
42.	alleys
43.	man-cain
45.	dreams
48.	buffet
49.	Making
50.	See
51.	God's Throne
52.	Allow Us
53.	Honey
54.	Sing
55.	I'm a Poet
56.	Ode to a Flock
57.	Sin factory
58.	ode to diablo's enfant terrible
59.	Springs
60.	iron chain
61.	Mist
62.	Debt Basket
63.	Arm on Fire
64.	Dance

65.	golden chalice
67.	ode to diablo's ancestry
69.	granite shell
70.	ode to diablo
71.	white flower
73.	Old Flute
74.	Worship
75.	Warden
77.	Cold Moon
79.	Flowers
81.	Alone Before a Mirror
82.	hourglass
83.	I Said
84.	You May be of Delilah's Ilk
85.	Ode to Cores
87.	ode to diablo's candy shit
89.	nests
90.	Ode to a Birth Name
91.	Photographs with a Gagged Mouth
92.	The Creed
93.	God
94.	Alone
95.	Humanimals
96.	Winged Glories
97.	A Photograph of Whispers between Rugged Mud Walls
98.	Ars Poetica
99.	Believe Me, I Did Not Prepare For Your Death
101.	Now
102.	an elegy for a pig's shit
104.	Acknowledgments
105.	Author Biography

Prologue

This collection of poems journals the poet's transition from darkness into light. The author talks of his coming into the world many years after his birth. Such conversion is what he calls a brewing dawn. The resurrection from despair into hope, faith in God and arrangements for a journey into a brighter light, are wielded by the poems. The author tells his story using various themes, in a familiar manner, yet some of the pieces spell the exact environs of the author. Some poems carry the writer's attempts to brighten the way towards hope, for others.

For my son, Athiei Marial Matueny.

Glow

Don't gag the glow
Of this love
Leaking into my soul.
This glow not rooted
In your core.

I have crossed lands
Wearing dark crowns
Where the sun should be.

Some lands chew sumptuous hours
Of potency
& throw us bones marrowed
Of spiceless malevolence.

Here, every hour is the pulse
Of God
& every word the leaf
& root to this living.

You cannot un-spit
My songs of true loving
And replace them with a gargantuan dynasty
Of pride,
And other little woundings of my leaping soul.

How a Firefly Dies

I never watched decay find a firefly.
I never watched the light dim
And turn on until the final dimming
Stretched into eternity,
at least for a firefly.

Here, I'm watching fireflies
Through the crack in the windowpane,
Yet unable to see my mind's lights
And its enclaves.
I cannot tell which firefly is shining
Its first light and which, its last.

national misery

national glory does not kill anywhere
but i cannot tell:
does national misery find a citizen
with a crown of hope or a bouquet of promises,
up the balcony of unborn dreams,
inside a beautiful city?

Sacrifice

I'm not sure of anything a creature can donate to the Creator.

The joy and the words one has & anything

One can sacrifice, belong to God.

Whatever reaction He accords one is also courtesy of Himself.

Neck

I asked a city poet about an art gallery
And he ended the conversation
With a self-portrait that holds
The artist's neck.

Hospital Lights

We giggled behind the mortuary.
The hospital lights
Lengthened our shadows
On the long grass lawn.
A newborn shrieked in the ward.
You were in a blue uniform
And I was tired of wearing any happiness
That did not jet into the sky
As a portrait of my inner bewilderments.
You said you hated the smell of formalin,
Because one laughs and it's all in one's throat.

Bites

My friend grabs a tsetse fly

Off his chin,

Beheads it and says:

'I created nothing that lives and bites'

history

there is no history without time
and time is its own history.

Fractions

According to the Scripture,
We were made fractions of God
But a stolen apple fractioned
Inside some people's mouths,
And we are now in a race,
To run into light or
Trip into brimstone furnace.
Where have you reached, so far?

tragedies

of all tragedies that can be forbidden,
let a poet love deeply.

boat

i like to go out first alone in my boat.
sometimes with sceptics ashore, whining
from purported pains along my path.
i prefer to welcome people who'd love to row
with me later, when i have mastered
my journey, and the boat is calmer
and set for the anchor.

love

i do not love running away
from you,
but if i do, it will be from the spiteful snares
you will plant.

coil

something in you
when hurt
folds into a ring
as does a millipede,
i am left checking
my sleeves for a stain of guilt

Yard

Anyone who plants and waters a plant
In his yard may not be punished for uprooting it,
But can be persuaded to let it grow.

Ode to Nothingness

Nothing can be enough to you
If your creator cannot suffice.
All the things that have no creator
Have not given us any compliment
About nothingness.
All the things God created may not be enough
To buy Him.

*

You can be given beauty and the blindness to see it.

*

I dread to say *us* when I am to be mentioned alongside God
—I do not know my proportion in that sum.
I also dread to say God and I,
Yet He accompanies everything.

*

You can only reward God best
By giving Him Himself.

*

By show of hands, who understands
The spoils and losses of being a creator?

*

Like… how did we arrive here?

*

Like… nothingness is a creature,
And we should be grateful for it.

*

Whatever wounds we have are somehow works of God.

*

Most of you are not our creators,
We therefore summon you to act holy
Only towards those you created.

*

The pastor says: 'God has no profit doing injustice to anything'
The prophet says: 'My children, why have you shitted
In the oasis again? Where will you drink?'

*

Like who does not need mercy?
They need mercy most who did not create
This universe: all, except nothingness.

I Adore

I adore the quality in things
That are vital
But not everywhere
Singing their vitality.
God is not flying overhead, bragging
To people of the expanse of His craft;

Bees and people seldom advertise pure honey,
You rarely find a vendor shouting to people:
'Here's honey made
From the sweetest of hums'

Somehow

My love has been seeking
For a rainforest in the desert.
I promise myself to soak W
holly when I reach one spring.

Cloths

I believed in evolution
Until I did not see
Gorillas gradually walk into cities,
Wearing cloths
& speaking the languages of people.

Kites

Below marauding kites
& kestrels,
I am rubbing the blade of a piebald
Feather against my palm.

White birds fly from one cow to another.
The plain is no quietude,
I can hear its music:
The fish slap water with their tails,
The water lilies present
Their unwavering benevolence,
What years of wars cannot invent.

Soul

I desire love that waters my passion.
I keep away from things that tear love
Away from my soul, like I evade fire flames.

Ode to a Pull

This is probably why
We could not meet
Over a cup of tea.

I was rising higher,
To sun up
My spot in the sky,

While you were preparing
To pull the globe
Away from my soles.

Pine Trees in the Rain

'This rain will not soak the sun'
Said an old man.

What again?

'Above the clouds, there's no rain'

Where did I meet the white cloak
Caught by the rain?'

Some part of me looking at this rain
Wants it to pour happiness.

The rainwater prattles in a basin
By the door.

I cannot see clearly the white roofs
Behind the pine trees.
I cannot see the small town
And its quietude I love most.

I cannot catch the abundance of beauty
Not mine in the rain sliding off pine trees.

What again?
Pine leaves do not fall from the sky.

At Mulago Cancer Ward

What do people want me to tell them now?
In front of me is a line of various cancer wards.
The doctors hurried in the amber light
Of this morning.
A young woman on a stretcher
Has been wailing to pain.
'How many days?'
I ask the doctor.
'Two painful months'
'Brought a case?'
'No!'
'I arrived here for a workshop
With the American Cancer Society'

Why Did You Let Them Tell You

That I hate the rains that wet the green shoots
And dry leaves of the forest?
Why did you let them tell you that I can pick one's joy
From the marrow of one's soul
And crumble it with my palm,
And throw a beautiful frown into a trash can
That may be full of crinkled things?

Yesterday, I saw it in their faces again:
That fury towards people who could love
Them, especially for wrongs they did not do.

They complain little insects dim my headlight,
And they cannot see me clearly.

Why did you let them tell you
That every air I breathe in
Is depriving the world of lungs?

Some are creeping here with hammers.
They say there is a light bulb above my head.

Why did you let them tell you
Its light is blurring sunshine,
And that there's also a levy for not knitting
The sun's sores?

I Sense Their Signals

There's joy in me not given out,
Good acquaintances not had,
Latent moments that could yield
Ecstasy.

Where should I spend them?
Now,
The sun ploughs its rays into trees,
Into porous black soil.

Now, July trees stand me   stand me.
I sense their signals of greenness
& peace.
Surely, I shall not spend
Things where they die.

Nothing

Nothing is enough when joy
Is needed in a heart every time.

Ode to Nationalism

Where you stand,
There is still an entire Nile.
There is a country and her wealthy
Endowments, handed to people by God.

I guess sense is far from you
To hear these things:
That there are nations in the hands
Of malevolent souls, wearied at their souls,
They bleed blood as black
As tar.

Lenses

for Beverly Nambozo Nsengiyunva

Over this plethora of dusks and dawns,
Cloud barracks of verses.
Let clouds shelter us from rain.
Let war tanks pass us by.
Let their appetite for war
Shake the earth beneath
Our capacity for beneficial cries,
As the words of benighted tyrants fly
Under our lenses as fighter jets & gunships.

Out of societal chaos,
Let blossom civilised ears to pool rebuke,
Where the flames flooding societal bones
Shall not find those who did not nurse the fire.

Goad the storms brewed in our pens
To blast, and fruit the pearls lost,
To harmful amputations of the living
Ocean of glory.
Shade our walk to human benevolence.

Diary Scribbles

20th July, 2021

    1
Keep nothing in my bottle
If all you donate is poison.

    2
I bet to be glad in a desert for the rainforest
That made me distinguish between the two.

    3
Wrap my soul up in many flags
Africa wears.
Wrap my soul in colourful wealth.

    4
I promise you, brother,
Whoever is waiting for us to give up
Will see the end of the world.

    5
Our home is what we did and are doing to it now.
Tomorrow, our home will be what we shall do to it.

Passions with a War Veteran

He asked what my passion was, and I said 'poetry'
He mentioned a genius friend he called S.G.,
His real name withheld.
S.G. by his account wanted to study at University of Oxford,
And after that, work his way to be S.G. of the United Nations.
He loved gin & co. After a few years, he walked barefooted
Around bars.

'Yesterday, at his funeral, we read an elegy from one poet
Who studied at University of Oxford', he said.

Just Watch Me

Just watch me, let my dream swallow me,
Like I'm making a coat of the Pacific Ocean
I can never distil.
Watch me have a dream most are afraid to think.
Don't dare say, 'what a waste of a dream!'

Moths

'Where do moths stay before I switch
On the lights?'
He raised a note titled 'In the Dark'
'Where do evil people stay before creation?'
He raised a dark cardboard with 'Half inside the Devil'
Chalked on.

Diabolism

There is a portion of diabolism
Wherever pure love is not enough.

The Universe

Sometimes a cage
The universe is just so vast
We ought to think we are free.
   doesn't end
Complete freedom ends
Where infinity does not end.
   freedom.
Our inability to travel the entire universe
Should not count as lack of freedom.

Audition

In the damp Nile Valley,
The water lilies and the flowing water
Are also not products of destruction.

*

Whatever a nation hungers to grow
With war does not bear a country
& its wealth.

*

In the last war,
The bombs fell and I watched a national lizard
Slip into a hole in a tree
& my love shook.
The lords of war kept tending the buds
Of misery,
Their phoney smiles, cleaned of the desire for true peace,
They audition on national TV.

*

I tell you, some of us did not aid in that gunfire.
We did not blow any bugle,
We did not make any war cry,
Yet soldiers ransacked our city.
I tell you, the tanker blocked the way to my favourite bakery.
I tell you, there were soldiers where the cinema was.
I tell you, we made no profits out of that war.

Soothing

After I met a few cruel souls,
I began to desire soothing souls,
I began to laud my pain
As the other route to discovery.

Winged by Time

Once, I started to sculpt a poem
Then it hardened so much
My knife became blunt.
I put it down formed by a portion,
Like a Kanye West smile paused
Before it bloomed.
Two days later, it flew into the sky
Now winged by time.

Aroma

Do not follow my shit
Into the toilet.
Do not complain about how hard
It is or how horrible it stinks.
You should, if you asked me,
First recall the savoury meal
It was made from
& smell the first aroma it gave off.

Place

      1

The place of origin

Of the best peace is in the womb

Of beautiful nature.

      2

The company of trees

By the river is a wordless conversation

And my soul speaks back.

      3

Why threaten me with war

When I am prepared to reject it?

Ode to the Maker of the Nile

Yours is a glitter spat from your core,
So full of life the sun glides off
Its face & washes off my sadness
Into a crown of water-lilies.

In the belly of earth, dinosaurs
Are already crowned with dust,
Close to the joys of dead dictators.

Pompous feet of past explorers
Could not divert her flow,
So, what passes through her tail
Swims out of her mouth.
You cannot shed tears
For rivers excavated as fossils,
Because from Your abundance
You have no store for lament,
Yet for folks that gift to darkness, souls,
You toot your dogma.

Maker of light,
We are sometimes rowdy passengers,
But we give You the boat,
For only You can row us
To the root of glorious time.

alleys

hurl
nectar-scented
waves
to this wind
blooms of the plain
my nostrils are your alleys

man-cain

bits of hope
drawn with these our souls
we sip from abundant wells

the disappointments
we cannot explain to newborns
who cry when nipples miss their lips

the queries we did not
make that hang at our necks
like goitre balls

the mistakes our ancestors could not undo
that they did not tell us their children

the abundant love doled to us
on a superfluous charity
that we are too hungry to take

the abels we felled
out of jealousy

the goats we sacrificed
for which we did not get rain

the grains we sowed for something
we did not reap

the winds that waved
our red-blooded flag
we did not kiss

all hang down
my throat like lumps
of salt

dreams

charred walls
curve around ashes

mesh of footprints of the last dance
to gunshot rhythm

air filled with breath
of ammoniac cartridges

rows of mass graves
sometimes mistaken for hills
upon red earth

priests drowned
in baptism water

oiled bones
outside ghost dwellings

bullets sunken
in dust

hopeful din
in melancholic
        silences

dust white upon ribs
of refugee kids

red-blooded
flags

abundant absences
& insufficient presences

potbellies
and hunger ulcers

wounded souls
and fat vultures

vicious warlords
and bishops
sharing the last supper

crosses and guns
roses and daggers

silhouettes of children
playing by the banks
of the Nile at sunset

ears clogged with
crude oil

poverty-sharpened tongues

a nation hides dreams
in her belly
dreams so alive they can
eternally birth
other dreams.

buffet

i reject your buffet of spiced poisons,
first, because i love myself
secondly, i desire to love after here,
things of nourishing beauty.

Making

Seated right at God's feet,
We keep making chains
& hanging them upon our shoulders
as insignia.

God keeps scolding:
"Get rid of all those chains
Of sins, my children, because the devil
Will use them to tie you up.
This is because I care.
This is because the devil
Did not create you!"

See

I'm to erase that which I see
See what we both watch and love.
I'm to undo my inner pictures of you
And bear only the good side,
To wed endless peace to both of us.

God's Throne

Every soul comes with the throne
Of God, grandiose and welcoming
Until when sat upon by say, horned monsters
Pooping demon-babes and rowdy hooligans
God has to choose where to sit
Which can be in another soul
Left intact.

Allow Us

Allow us to commend bees
For the honey they have made.
Do not sing its taste to us,
We may have different taste buds.

Honey

Do not be honey dissolved
In their acids.
Always, let your oceans tide
To meet their deserts.

Sing

I sing from the deep wells of my soul.
What then will I sing
If my soul is filled with fire?

I'm a Poet

I'm a poet:
I hunger much for love.
Flood me with true loving.
You won't easily grow a water lily
In a desert.

I'm a poet:
I cannot run senseless & mechanical,
Like a truck carrying scented flowers
To a funeral.

Ode to a Flock

I have shown you the route
To Me,
So why, my children,
Are you aiding the wolf
In finding your flock
Why are you a guide
In helping him find you?

Sin factory

You labour hard at sin factory
Making lots of futility
While in your promised land
Abundances of viable glories flood.

ode to diablo's enfant terrible

small rascal, i own it all.
so, I keep the fireball
i send rolling into your small stall.
you scamper wildly but hit a wall
& wish I did not pick of war
from the store of benevolent wares.

Springs

I keep locked inside me
Sprouting springs
Of potencies,
When before me
Some beings pour swathes
Of scorching lava.

iron chain

i once sat with them around
the same familial bonfire
sharing stories
of a valiant ancestry
before they sucked sweet sap
from my living

but only you i do not know
i also do not know where you picked this red-hot
iron chain you want us to pull

Mist

I know who you are,

Yet you live drenched

In rotting leaves of vain history.

Your ears are so many

You can no longer hear

The whispers

Of this beautiful mystery

Misting inside me,

& the blue clouds ungathering

Above me.

Listening to my inner songs,

I woo the seasons to melt

The granite door

Between our ships,

Sailing towards one another

Upon the ocean of time,

& the chirps of the budding

Dawns, at the root

Of a swaggering dream.

What you are feels like all the souls in the world

Giggling under a rising full moon.

Debt Basket

God's mercy to me
Feels like a fall paused
Or breath warred back
Into a dead body.

Some mercy I give
Has grudge standing
Outside the chapel
Of joy,
Holding open the debt
Basket.

I take a true smile
To be a greater form
Of forgiveness,
Especially when it spreads
Where desolation should reign.

Arm on Fire

In the land of the beasts,
One can best rule
Those with no wings to fly
& Ones who are not fast
Enough to get away.
More, if a bird perches upon
A despotic arm on fire.

So far in this land,
Owned by wolves
Who fill their bellies
And mistake them
For everybody's,
The pipe to fruition
Is clogged with blooded
Crude oil.
Their pompous words of fatal
Hope & domineering anarchy
Leap over leaking
Veins of a potent nationhood.

Dance

I lament every camouflage
For truth.

I lament every love slaughtered
And sprinkled on bread.

I lament when there's no reflection for my mind:
the place I wish to rear in wonder & true love.

There's no lament for a good
Dance...
At my first dance,
    After my brother died,
My friend said it wasn't just a dance.

He said He saw grief somersault
    Over verses of Kendrick Lamar.
    He said: you are a broken man
Inside a broken country,
    And the music is glueing
Your soul to the quietude
Of God.
I lament the joys I can't tether.

golden chalice

before you speak,
i spill every fall
offered in a golden chalice
& some morsels the hours bore through
me holes to anchor time.

look, the mirrors i have
aren't designed to dress
naked lies of benighted
charlatans.

i do not live in pride-land
to poke my golden tongue
into the cores of many suns
i did not create.

before you speak,
a finger in hot water
deserves to be seen as it is.

before you speak,
i am not the brewer
of dawns
but i welcome the hairs
of their tails with hymnal
solemness.

before you speak,

i drink from the springs

of God's mercy

& spread out my dreams

for the night to watch over.

ode to diablo's ancestry

here, i'm the king of refusals:
you to have to collect your etherising
fart
     you label to people as perfume.

my river is so made of sunlight
to be tainted by fleeting nights.

i'm a harvest of dawns
not yet gained,

so, you can now collect
your black assembly
of seatless royalties.

all your hunt is a fruiting of futility,
all because i'm everywhere.

flee to your decaying dynasty
of festive maggots,

because again, i'm king,
and here, you cannot stop
a Nile you did not drill.

leave that water, rascals.
don't touch that sun, rascals.

all i offer you is a terrified flight,
which i can also take away,
if you delay.

granite shell

i have crossed
the ocean of many thirsts.

i have outgrown the granite
shell that kept
me warm.

i have teleported into the glories
    of tomorrow.

ode to diablo

i was inside God
   when the blade of fire
      struck you here.

i'm all conquering,
and you, you're
   the grain of dust
upon my royal attire
the winds replace.

i snore the fire that melts
the tongue of rancour
& send scattering all your white-eyed children,
nocturnal vipers
   of the broken tablet.

you lurk and dream
for the hour my hauntings
will cease,
but i forever giggle my fires
into the darkness
of your malevolent
living.

white flower

> *for Hauwa Liman*

are you still there,
a white flower

from green?

our searchlights
are only awake enough

to unveil our hands,
filled with feasts

strung by political
rallies.

the government
is holding

a fleshy bone
in its mouth
to pull one breath

back
into the national
anthem.

hear our song,
the potency of wings

waxed to a statue
upon a pedestal
of dawn.

Old Flute

The season of hope has breathed:
I disembowelled my gun of its new seeds
And cut out its trigger.
The old flute, holes netted
By cobwebs
I cleaned and smeared with oil.

In April, came the rains I did not summon yet desired.
I welcomed the colours of bluebells and lotuses.
I asked for more downpour to the arid lands of my spirit
& that thorns will not sprout
From the dark humus of my soul.

Worship

Humans deserve to be truly loved,
Not worshipped.
Worship is a thing only for God.

Warden

1
By the way,
Who has this dream
Sucking blood from the heart
Of its bearer?

2
So I can know,
Who has this dream
That wears a golden crown
Of vanity and shits among
God's flowers?

3
And whose dream is this one
Carrying upon its shoulders
A boulder that can twice crush
Its holder?

4
Again,
Whose dream is this one
Fast forwarding its perceiver
 Into a strange desert,
Unprepared and with no water?

5
Who has this dream
Mending the cracks in its ship &
Welding rainbows against
A destructive homecoming?

6

I do not know this dream:

A wild kite grabbing morsels

From hands of little children.

7

I also do not recognise this dream

 fast on a horse away from God.

8

I accept blame for any beauty

That goes past me

While I slumber into one dream

I can't weave into a land

Of green plains and beautiful springs.

9

You cannot just overlook

My gigantic grievances

Just to highlight your small

& futile wants.

Cold Moon

I didn't create myself,
So here, I order the moon
Cold

My ancestral anthems carry
Spears that fly through people.
Some days, I feel the songs evade me.
Some days, I feel myself flinching
From the songs.

Speak,
I have not yet chosen spears
Over a beautiful floodplain
Reigned upon by a cold moon.

First, I want the moon cold
And cleansed of decay.
I want a calabash full
Of light.

I don't know what I can do
With your deity's scentless twilight,
When I bathe in cold milk
Upon the lapse of the Creator,
Seated right in the sun's cores.

Speak,

Here, I can't bite a block of butter minus
His grace.
Here, I can breathe in amniotic lava.

Flowers

If You hide other presences,
Show me what I flower.
I have grown certain things I can't touch,
That from the splash of sunlight leave mystery behind:
Some things that gift swarms of stings.
The leaves of trees are painting their many colours
And people carry home
Harvests of most things I don't bear.
I was once shown beautiful
Flowers of a poisonous tree
And where under it a rabbit
Died from a bee's sting.

I can't wholly understand you &
I can't wholly understand myself more.
I'm clearly tired of rearing my desires.
One second, they're in the water cooling off and shuffling
Into the deep,
The next, they are scooping
Wildfires with grass baskets.

Sometimes, I forget and drill holes into the ship
That You say will carry me to Miracle Land,
Just to make it lighter.
Sometimes, I'm filling with honey a holed up container.

I think there could have been You

And your assembly,

& only flowers

& only rains

& only rivers.

Why give misery a chance?

Why do we need suffering?

My own living

Is so much a miracle,

I sometimes take it for granted.

I think it blasphemous to understand it.

Alone Before a Mirror

Alone before a mirror
I say to myself:
"The noise you cannot hear
Is God minting abundant beauty
Your eyes cannot cage.

The crowd is outside buttering
Its cheers.
Drown in the mirror
This frown you flaunt
With ostrich feathers
Upon its head.
You're not being swallowed
In anyone's mind"

I open the curtains to the black
Trees and the moon glittering
Above them.
The moon cannot know
I'm by a portion its mirror.
But I can say in this solitude
The moon is one of my companions.

hourglass

i search
for a flood of joy
      in the abundance of harmless abandonment.

my rejections,
  i don't command to slice
the womb
  of things i endear.

my desires
  lick every hourglass
that never empties of good harmony with oneself.

my acceptances spell:
whatever i love
i love it for whatever i love.

there's no cutting
a fruit of me
for a show.
there's no party for me
for falling
off the scalp
of peace.

I Said

I said nothing about the snake's bones by a dirt road.

I said nothing about most of those wars.
What do I have in anyone's war?

I told myself nothing that could make me sad.
Now, I said nothing that'd make anyone sad.

I said nothing about history.
Why would history just be talked about in its absence?

I said nothing about the morning glories at my door.
I can also hear beauty in quietude.

I said nothing about you and some of your wants
& how they can choke you to survival before you invent other wants.

I said nothing about nothing.
I said nothing about everything I said.

I just can't be the host and the guest.

You May be of Delilah's Ilk

If you peel off your skin
To cover from coldness
People seated around
Their own bonfire.

If you break down your fortress
To build the fire
That burns down your kingdom.

Ode to Cores

I won't allow
The beautiful cores
Of my inner wounds
To soothe your golden
Ring,
Because I have grown
Out of them an entire field
Of flowering hope.

I won't allow you
To pick my specks
And pin them to the sky,
In attempts to brighten yours,
Because they complete
The miracle that I am.

I won't allow you
To replace the giggle
In my throat,
Because you can't brew
The exact joy I can make.

I won't allow you
To feel my pain,
Because your nerves
May not accurately feel mine.

I won't give you the keys
Into my mind;
I'm afraid you may get lost
Or rear it in menace.

ode to diablo's candy shit

there's a certain decor in things
i reject,
a decor others may not
see with my eyes.

i eschew your golden
lies.
i eschew your pearls
lining my hungers
for jewellery.

boy, i want the storm
to whirl you away with my shit.
boy, i want the tongue behind
thunder.

look at the forest of pine trees
before me.
look at the sky churning an aurora borealis.
in many things my rejection found joyous futility.

look at yourself:
some restless squirrel
jumping around &
somersaulting over heads of sleeping priests.
look at yourself working
over time,

with the churches closed.

look at yourself having no place to close.

there's no communion
in your chalice.
there's no wine in your cup.
there's no breath of fire inside your lungs.
you own nothing you created.

nests

now,
a storm
    nestles
      outside
nests.

the nerves of lightning,

   they are neither hairs
   nor twigs.
upon the green grass, my dim shadow tints leaves.
the artwork of God is a miracle.
the artwork of God is for those who can see or feel it.

Ode to a Birth Name

I command my right
To give any birth name
To any joy in the core of my wound.
  *

You cannot just miss
To announce the beauty
In other people's scars.
  *

I did not ask you to remind me
Of the dry season's burnt ashes
Where now stand green trees
& birds upon their branches.

Photographs with a Gagged Mouth

     1
We watched a viper slide into a hole,
Then clogged the hole with stones,
To save the many it may bite.
     2
That part of the Nile closer to the delta
Runs slower, muddied mainly by the load
Cleaned off its banks.

The Creed

The stars are not spread out at night as white grains on a black sheet
Each star shines from its locus
The sun can burn anything close, except what burns to exist
The space we shall never reach is the beginning of infinity

God

Your abundant mercy,

Will bless my wanting the presence of the universe,

Will let me be the fire water will not quench.

Alone

When with myself
I am less offended.
When with God
I am not alone,
Back in Eden.

Humanimals

We shall not share much with animals:
If we don't lust to prey on our kind
Like the carnivores,
If we do not host the paroxysm of jealousy
As of a goat knocking another, for standing
Where it is supposed to stand,
If we cannot be leeches tucked to skins
That do not belong to us.

Winged Glories

Now, I am free enough to say
My urine after antibiotic therapy
Wipes out bacteria in the toilet tub.
The paper I write on means
A tree has been stopped
From bearing other trees.

Yes, I'm here, where some rivers
Have been made crossable
And the moon not dark.

The bloodless sun torches freely
Past bodies teleporting into God's possible
Conversation of another garden
Toured by winged glories and absent decays.

A Photograph of Whispers between Rugged Mud Walls

Wholly inside my skin,
Dreams packed and a matchstick lit,
I wait if the rugged mud walls
        Will womb me in.
All those nine months,
If I had workable suspicions
        They were all plotting
To scrub laughter off tree barks,
The universe may again take His voice
To weave fire   into a flower.
    Cuddle.
Whichever, I shall still hug the night,
        My hands as light as God's
        Search for Himself
In a sack filled with mud.
My mouth dripping cold whispers,
He will know when I collect basketfuls
        Of true pain and sculpt it into a statue,
        Just like I plot to pour emptiness
        Out of clay pots.
He will know how between flooded days
Filled with broken arks and givable rainbows,
When full of myself, I can still float,
When Mother Earth is still coarse to wash down
        With things doused in syrups.

Ars Poetica

There will be neither tears nor giggles
            In poetry
         Until pens
              Begin to shed real drops & joys
                  That can sprout
                          Mountains on blank pages.

Believe Me, I Did Not Prepare For Your Death

for Malual Matueny, murdered on 28th March, 2014

The plains in *Wunthou* still flood
With the fall of rains.
You will find their white-flowered faces
                When you return,
And that I am flooded by raging waves
Of injustice.

I also stand immersed in guilt not mine,
For letting your parents
Teach me only how to: keep hunger
                In my belly but never on my face;
Cross a chain of ants
                My hands clutching my balls;

  Urinate in the river
                    When a crocodile's head sprouts;
Let seeds decide to germinate.

                I forgot all about mourning,
The knack of turning tears into sweet songs
And moans into an orchestra of singing flutes.

Worse, I have no sweet name for malicious murder.
The audience,   their skins are shrinking with loathing
—They want it entertaining.

So calm child of one birth,

My mourning has been satisfactorily boring,

                      All because I did not prepare for your death.

Now

Now, here's a lizard's tail
Moist with blood at my door.
I do not have to worry much
Perhaps, the owner forgot it
Or was despotically given pain
And has no more tail to lose.

an elegy for a pig's shit

the fact that you and i
next-yard neighbour
share the dark odour
of pig ordure for a long time
but taste and smell never together
the flavour of your fried pork
is to my appetite an endeavour
not in favour of the tastiness of charity's flavour

Acknowledgments

I'm grateful to fellow poet and friend, *Dzikamayi Chando*, as well as my dear friends: *Lino Mabor Maker Nyariel, Puorchien Matueny Makeny, Maker Maker Mading* and *Lang Mayang Majoch,* for their unwavering support and advice throughout the process of writing and publishing this book.

Author Biography

Marial Awendit is a South Sudanese poet, essayist and songwriter. He is widely published in various literary magazines and anthologies:

Brittle Paper

Kalahari Review

African Writer Magazine

Ramchiel Magazine

CreatePreneurAfrica

Eboquills

Praxis Magazine

Garden of Poems

Songs of the Nile

the Best New African Poets Anthology

Elsewhere poetry.

He is the author of the poetry chapbook, *The Night Does Not Drown Us*, Babishai-Niwe Poetry Foundation

His debut poetry collection, *Keeping the Sun Secret*, Mwanaka Media and Publishing Ltd.

Marial won the *2016 South Sudan Youth Talent Award* for the category of Best Poet and the *2018 Babishai Niwe Poetry Award*.

www.ingramcontent.com/pod-product-compliance
Lightning Source LLC
Chambersburg PA
CBHW021443080526
44588CB00009B/662